The Sun at Midnight

AF624802

CarLa Howard

BookLeaf Publishing

Presentation by *BookLeaf Publishing*

Web: www.bookleafpub.com

E-mail: info@bookleafpub.com

ISBN: 9789357442916

First edition 2023

To my Sun... The truth of you is my muse

PREFACE

Imagine a world where the sun appears at Midnight. In the darkest hour,
the brightest star appears in the form of love poems, romantic and erotic stanzas that capture your heart and maybe even your breath...pulling you into a sensual solar flare.

The Evidence

Existentially a goddess
Her soul was proof of life

Snatched

She no longer belonged
To Herself

Sacrificed
in the name of
Self Care.
Her greed, and the need to feed it
Had taken over

Not able to deny herself
Any longer
Of the many deaths she
Sought to die upon him
She transitioned
Willingly

Offered her spirit to the
Highest Bidder
And He Won
She couldn't

afford herself
When the stakes were high
So she folded

They agreed to meeting
Next Lifetime
Convinced they'd find each other
In any dimension
So
They jumped

Felt feathers become
Skin where dorsal
Wings had been
They were mostly Human

Time had its way and
Love got lost In translation
Settled in the distant corners of
These new minds
A cobweb of remembrance
Collecting like dust,
Eyes of heaven
Blind

The ancestral winds
Blew their four horns
Announcing
A change of

Seasons

Impervious to
Imperfection
Their union
Was nothing
Shy of
Celestial

He belonged inside her
Their connection was
That which could hold objects
Together
And allowed spirit molecules
To compound
Into flesh

This connection
Was Life
Was the reason
Bees pollinated
And trees gave way
To Bearing fruit
This connection came with
Urgency

When he pushed deep
Into her vortex
She knew the ocean
Would break from
The clouds

His presence held
Her attention like
Moses holding back
The Red Sea

A black Isrealite
With godliness
In his manliness
Godliness
Within his reach

A prophecy was fulfilled as
He sent stars into her
Magellanic spiral

Precipitation dripping
From the solar system within her
Rainbows created as her chakras
Aligned in Order
Her lotus had opened to the Sun

The elevation came immediately
Combined pleasure propelling them both
Into the Stratosphere
The requirement to breathe with intention
Pressing it's insistence upon
Their lungs
Their hearts found a new way of beating
That spoke Unity
Like a foreign forgotten language
Evidence
They had once
Been lovers in Heaven

Kiss of Life

His kiss
Is prayer
Is life
Is floatation device
When the flood is drowning me in its currents
It's currency
Paid tithes
Subscription to the Most High
It's spell speak
And black majick
It's a feather in my mojo bag
It's a pep in my step
And the drop of dew that clings to morning leaves
When the day is new

My lips part to welcome
His completion
Inside my Journey
Kisses that merge two ancestral families
His kiss unburies me
Removes the day's carbon dioxide
And replenishes my oxygen
Breaths exchanged
Until his kisses become my kisses

And my kisses
Elevate his vibe
Until he's ringing in the right frequency
Kissed while silent language
Formats in the basis of his
Kundalini
My kisses are ceremony
And a lit white candle
My kisses contain the secrets
Of the moon's recipes
And a promise of a meal fit
For a king

I taste like forever
He tastes like
I can never live
Without his lips
We kiss
Like sinners
Finding
Salvation
In
Putting our
Mouths together
Like two is always better
Than one
Like a kiss is
The only thing
We'll ever
NEED

The Sun at Midnight

You first came to me in the color crimson
Your red hues leaking into my conscious
Etching a silhouette of your presence in the perimeter of my mind
Had I found you?
My twin flame?
Your name
full of possibilities danced in my mouth
And whenever we spoke in passing
My heart started galloping
Like a wild horse racing
The sands of time
Something about you screamed
Come find me
I knew you were to be mine
Images of us in Romance
Haunted the hallows of my heart
And permeated my third eye's view
Silently this love grew to be true
Opportunity intersected with time
And the arrows in my quiver were
Primed
This wouldn't be target practice
As your walls were high
I had to hit your mind

Like a bullseye…
Then I saw the shine
A brilliance illuminating
From deep within your soul
Recognized like
You were my intended lover from
A lifetime ago
My attention to you more attentive than a shadow
Where ever you Gogh
My heart will Gogh
Your loving warmth and mental glow
Familiar like a memorized constellation
I had seen in the skies of a starry night
Brighter than Quasar
You will always be my perfect
Sun at Midnight

Sunburn

This glow
has spread
It's radiance
On my skin
Kisses my bronze
And makes good love
To my melanin
The brilliance of your love
Easing its
Way down my Yellow Brick Road

Life slid some oil
To my bones
And Courage
Gives me the heart
Of a Lion
So
Wildly I Roar
I am a woman
Adored
I call it Wizardry
That which whirlwinds
My soul to a place I call home
While gazing into
Your galaxy

I welcome the stars to
Come dance in my eyes
The twinkle is something
Sirius
Mysterious and Mystical
Mythical
Like a goddess
You've never seen before
But pray to because
You believe in

The universe has a womb in
My irises for you to
Conceive in
Come
Put your seeds in
My mind

Cause what is Mine
Is for me
And I get everything

Paid like monthly
Utilities
To keep the lights shining brightly
When the rest of the world
Sits dimly

In its own darkness
It's heartless to
Think
Everybody could afford
This
They can't

Elevator opened doors
For elevation
But only took us to the third floor
Until we decided
That's what the stairs are for
Until then it was just a try
Not a climb
But you get me higher
By nosediving deep
Into my mind
To get to the bottom of this

And I know that he knows my ass is his

That's why he
Has my body mentally charted
Categorized by its responding parts
The weight of my atomic
mass
Memorized
Has tasted the elements
Of my being

Knows the compound
Of my ocean
Like a Marine
But he's more nautilus
He lifts me
Easily
Has the inertia to
Move me mentally
I'm not Heavy
Inside his heart

Yet every time I
Speak his name
I make his ventricles
Tickle
And his atria sneeze
He's allergic to the absence of me
So his pulse beats
Accordingly
In accord with me
Our breathing the epitome
Of Reciprocity

Organically he grows
In me
Roots dug so deep in me
I'm a part of his history
A King and his Queen
That makes us family

Write my name
On his life tree
I decided I'm not
Deciduous
I'm never leaving
My feelings to another man to be raked
Over and Bagged
Now I understand Etta
When she Sang At Last

I promise to make it Last Forever
So I'ma be sweatin Keith
harder than an out of shape
Athlete
With free agency
He'll never be on the bench with me

We're not aging see
Time is on some
Benjamin Button stunting
I don't call him my Baby for
Nothin
I got that good milk
He knows that Similac be frontin
You see My skin tells the truth better
That good love is the Fountain of Youth
And the water is only getting wetter

So we learned to swim
Upstream against
The flow of distance
Space has not the capacity
In this instance
To keep me from seeing Distal
Our future manifesting
Where prayers are heard
In the belly of a crystal
He has me altering
My altar
To make room for the
Ultimate offering
Given Freely
He lets me be
Me
I never ring off tone
When he's around
I resonate loudly
Like a singing bowl
Without saying a sound
The melody is in my glow
He is the undertone to my Brown

Seven

This is on seven
This is like heaven
was a place from which some god looked down
And said these two are infinitely bound
So he made us 1 and 1
Glow of the Moon reflecting the Sun

Like 11:11
That's an angel number
But even wings wouldn't let me
fly or hover
Any higher than you get me
And you get me completely
Received me as I should be
Finish sentences I haven't even begun
One divided by two bodies is still one
We are that new math
Our whole selves still only equal to half
Until we plus our love through reciprocation
We are the perfect equation

You have to be from the same nucleus
From which I departed
We are from the same star
Thus we are equal hearted

Me in the North
And you're Southern charted
That makes us bipolar
Opposites but like identical twins
In the mirror we flame
You are the breath under my name
I am the energy that you sustain
Not destiny nor fate lends to the chance
That we was crafted in spiritual hands
Fused back together as part of a plan
I know we ain't brand new
First kisses aren't supposed to feel like deja vu
Even before my lips had been on you
How true that souls recognize souls
By the vibes they wear like clothes
That day by the Nile we was chose
To be together
It took a lifetime to find you again but
We are here now so whatever
Infinity keeps repeating Us
Energy is neither created nor destroyed
So love I trust
That we just transferred to this Universe
So we could continue what we started
The healing of our presence
Cathartic

My soul sent to light on your skin like a
butterfly

Fluttered into your reality like a dream
you drift into
And as I
Tasted you with my proboscis
I remembered
I missed this
Had found a way to cross the distance
Millenniums were dimensionless
But the visions relentless
Until in my waking hour
I conjured your soul to me
Thus claiming my power
10th to the Sun
Your fire devoured
And soaked into my aura
As your essence ran through me
Shaking me to my core
What had been undiscovered
Was never more lost to me
Planetary alignment
Achieved in the galaxy
Returned to my axis as Queen
And you as ruler
An effigy
Of the word destiny
The epitome
Of the better half of me
The prototype
Of manifesting

Completion
In godly terms
The number of days
Our world turned
While we created
Breathed life
Until our souls changed
Remembered who we used to be
So we could find our
Way to Becoming
Our elevated selves

And that is on seven

The Secret Life of Crystals

When you engulf me in your Carnelian arms
Your Amber chest becomes the perfect place
To rest my Lapis Luzuli when I need to snooze
You love my blues
But never give them to me
Unless it's in gift of our love language
Of the poets stone
Sodalite makes me heavy with
Words like
"I love you"
Throat chakra
clearing as my
Rose Quartz
Blooms open

Resting in the presence
Of your black onyx
Grounds me
Allows me to embrace
The femininity of
My moon stone
Polished Amazonite
Shining
My thoughts clear as Quartz
With my Topaz legs wrapped around you

I stare into your Tiger's Eye
Feeling the Jasper of tranquility ease through me
You find me like a Diamond beautified
My clarity held in your hand
All facets appreciated
When you embrace me in gold
And beckon me to sit at your right side
My kisses drip from my Ruby lips
Speaking words of Amethyst
Bestow royalty to your third eye
And elevate your Citrine mind
We are the natural resources of the land
Earth's Jewels
Draped in Melanated
Cloaks
Suspended in Love's Dimension

Coffee

If-
You are a consistent coffee drinker
Not because you are addicted to
The caffeinated affects
but because
You like coffee
You can begin to understand
What his kiss is to me...
How it starts my day
How one sip is never the only sip,
I gotta finish the cup
How he is savored
Enjoyed
Pleasing to not just my mouth
But my other senses as well

You may have an idea
That a good cup of coffee
Like a good kiss
Can change
Your outlook for the day
You might begin to
Understand how easily
The mmmm sound slides
From me

How he elicits
That sounds from somewhere
Deep and
unintentional
A soul approval
Because I just enjoy
His coffee
I mean his kisses
I mean his kisses are addictive
And I love
When he percolates his lips
And brews for me
When his heat hits my face
And I know I will taste
Exactly what I want in my day
I want to drink him up
Cup by delicious cup
I know you understand
If-
you are a
Coffee drinker

The Gift

You've changed me
Put meaning in places that
Previously didnt make cents
Did dime bag division
Subtracting the opinion of those
That can't claim me
Until nothing was left except
Their two pennies
The cost of a thought that means
Nothing laying at the bottom of the water
I wish them well
But you
wish me better
Prayed over me
With verbal alchemy
Injecting
Your own energy into my god body
Let's stay together
Be a Universal emblem
The symbol for love
Weighted on Atomic charts
As the lightest compound
An essential mineral
And good for my heart
My etheric self returns to you nightly

In our reality
Our waking hours are the dream
Time holds no boundaries is what it would seem
When you breathe your words into me
Layers sloughed from my walls until all is raw
Bared and exposed you read me
I say nothing
The scribblings of elementary prone men erased
to be replaced by the esoteric
Philosophy
You write on me so deeply
Inscribe spiritual ceremony
We know the freedom found in our Ancestors'
bleeding
They also craved
Knew the only way to be eternally bound was to
taste the DNA
Of the stars
So they held their heads back
And let the skies leak into their mouths
So when you spit
constellations gather and
The Moon cries
Remembers the lullabies of
Her younger self
Your words are your wealth
You conjure spells
Work majick
That changes me

In the twinkling of
My third eye
Kingdoms are built on the pronouns of
You and I
We be goddess and god
Our power wielded in pen swords
We can create or slay with
You my King
Are manifestation of the Gift

An opportunity others had but knew not what to do with...)

Musicality

Musicality
In the name of Love
Lemme pour my Sugar on you
Rock and roll these hips
Until I feel your dick
Jump
To the conclusion
Of my walls
If they wonder why
I walk this way
I'll blame it on the
emptying of your balls
I'm nothing
like a lady
No white wedding to claim
Face to face with me
lookin into the eye of the tiger
You can call Pussy
by her first name
Your heat surrounds me
Hungry like the wolf
You stalk your prey
I know your fire is next
Followed by your coldplay
We fall like cold rain

On a summer's day
Torrential
When I rock you like a hurricane
And sweep you into my
Center
Elemental
Nothing conventional
About us
We move up and down
Like love in an elevator
Until we both bust
Now I'm crying
Your name
Free Fallin from
Heaven's pearly gates
My broken wings
Replaced
By my beautiful legs
Wrapped around your waist
Hold me here tight
Suspended
In the air of tonight
While I look you
In your eyes
It's the end of the world as we know it
Our bodies signing our names to this covenant
You called me your Queen
Said my moans are a bohemian rhapsody
Your strokes like the beats of Rap City

Your hands played with my miss melody
I followed the chorus as you led me
Call us the Symphony
You Peter Piper piped her
But we ain't no Children's story
Get the message
I swallowed more kids than you left with
So I've babysat them until I spit this
Finally swallowed
When you promised me all your tomorrow's
We crossed the white lines
no forgettin we more than Friends
Ain't no half stepping
Only up in my guts gettin
Until 6 N the morning
You can rock the bells until the landlord is reportin
And if we hear a knock at the door
I'm yelling
Fuck Da police
We still recordin
I'm a microphone fiend
And my lips are escorting
Your next hit
Your final fix
You was talkin all that jazz
And all that shit
Until I put my jelly on you and Jammed on it

Now I'm ego tripping but you can Express yourself
But I'ma drink the formula
Til ain't none left

Purity Prayer

Purity Prayer

Dehydrated
Need for me under estimated
Apparently
And now you're requiring
My replenishing
To coherently
Think
Back to the last time we were together
I baptized you in my river
and called
You purified
Because I came
clean
You can't deny the
Need
You feel freed from
Life and die happily
 in my pool
Until
The greed sneaks up on you
And possesses you like a demon
Bears it's teeth and forces you to
Feed on me an'

The way you consume me has to be a form of cannibalism
And then
You injected me
Infected me
When you fed your sex to me
Now I feel it
Eating away at my sanity
Riddling my brain with constant thoughts
Of swallowing your cum
What a monster
I've become
Growling from deep in my esophageal cave
The voice of my crave
Yelling louder than the silence
That is in my belly when I'm not digesting your essence
This is nonsense
Was it me that was mistaken
How did I not account for and take in
The amount of ounces I was depleted from
The volume of your cum not coming to me
Quickly enough
to stave off this sickness
Of undickedness that has fallen upon me
I can't think coherently
Apparently I need
Your fluids
Hook me up

Intrapenisly
Drip
Your lactated solution
And solve this equation
Baby I'm sayin
I'm dehydrated
Recalculate the calibration
Of infusion
That you're choosin
to let me take in
Only you can
Rid me of this sin
Baptise me with
Your drops
So that I too
may be
Purified
Amen

My Lucky Daye

My Lucky Daye

I'm auto tuned to his tone
The bass of his voice
Works like a sonar when
He speaks life into his Home
I echo his reflection
His resonance rich like the
Renaissance
I hear only him
period
All other noise is dissonance
He composes me like sheet music
But plays my body like a singing bowl
I hum when he moves around the rim of my
hole
I mean my perimeter
Speaks me in perfect pentameter
Like an experienced poet with a lyrical gift
Sings me like a church hymn with
A sprit filled riff
Spits me like bars in a Rappers delight
And I'm drunk on his Cypher cause that's what
I'm drinking tonight
His Crown Royal in Shades of Black

I want shots of him poured from the back
He orders me to pour him wine
But not in a glass
He drinks directly from my winery
The rest spills down to my ass
Now the sheets are wet
He never lets me forget
How much of a glutton he can be
Told me he was greedy
And now I see
He crushes Grapes in side when he grinds and beats
10 strokes of dick
His merlot is mine
And his Riesling
I want to drink
All potential offspring
Swallow his seed
As a life offering
Let my body be the Altar
I'm not explaining or giving a reason
My truth never falters
He keeps me in moans and breath pants
though it's Sundress Season
At its peak
He expanded my Horizon
Had me proclaiming his praises
For a week
Oh my god is such a freak

Confession: In the key of life, he's never off key
We fit together like melody and harmony
Hard to explain what the dick do to me
But he knows how to get all of me
Every ounce
Every drop
Insists I give it all and
Only then does he stop
Releases his fingers grip
From his sweet choke
Tells my hips to
Roll some more
All because he knows
I want all the smoke.

A Whole New World

I crossed the Middle Passage of love
Rode the relationslave ship
Took me past my borders,
-cramped
This ain't my land.

Thinking I should've jumped overboard
To save myself
Drowning to save my sanity
Felt the whip sting on my back
The crack of men that lacked
navigational skills
Couldn't even guide themselves yet but still
smacked my skin, it stung but didn't break me

Now enter you, master of love levitation
You elevate me
like reiki
A new way of practicing old hoo doo

Can't say I didn't see it was you
Coming
Made my pineal gland tingle
You came to me in mugwort induced visions

Woodwormed your way
with room and time to spare
before we ever mingled
Offered gifts to my ancestors asking them do I
dare approach your heart
Not surprised that they answered that they had
led me here
To you.
Put you on my altar to alter our lives
If you invited me to enter

Words chanted
under the influence of moonlight
Star arranged alignment I was drunken with
Alliteration.
That is our abracadabra
Brown bodies bask in bare beauty before
beginning to be the beacon for black love
I thank the Universe for this opportunity
Manifestation as below,so above
Binding our rib's occupancy
Spell speak
Is what we whisper
Incantations inhaled
We conjure in whispered tones
Exhale spirit
When we breathe in moans

Show me your god body

So that I may serve
You fervently
Put you in my practice until perfected
Your lingam is the wand
My yoni the cauldron
Something is brewing
You provide the fire
My hips stir our potion
Waist beads add seasoning

I will climax liquid
Majick
And anoint you
My Chosen One
And our ancestors
Will Agree
Palm their old hands on wet drums
They know our rhythm
And dance to our beat

I Wrote your name on a bay leaf
and burned the ashes into the wind
You'll never be lost to me again
Cinnamon kisses to my lips like the last
ingredient added to a sweetening jar.
You are my honey.
My honey you are
like an old remedy
Natural and good for me

My manuka
My Shango
old god to my goddess
Liza to my Mawu
I create love with you
Infinitely
we are
Candles burnt
Down to the wick
Definitely
We are old majick

Magnetism

He’s so magnetic
That even my pen is attracted
I tried to retract it
But instead it
Corrected the refraction
And new words were
Reflected
On the back of my eye
I see what’s really going on
I know he’s so refreshing
That water swallows him up
For rehydration
Oceans drink his name by the moon full
A new measurement created to
Tell me how much make to add to my room
To take him all in
He’s more than a glassful
Let this poem be my testimony
A proof of a life that no longer
Belongs to me
Because I became a pocketful of Lunarbeam
In the shirt of a solar king
Celestial
He moves me

I’ve climbed mountains I didn’t know the name of
I’ve seen the other side
And coming down
Was worth the trek
For being at the bottom
Means another chance to go up
This time maybe it peaks higher
I said he makes me move
Do things I said I wouldn’t
and Some I
Doubted I could
Like finding light underneath a sky
That has closed its eyes
Simply by smiling at me
Possibility has become the bigger person
Dwarfs the uncertainty
That sometimes lurks at the back of my heart
peeking around the corner
To see if I’m alone
I’m not fooled
By this love affair my pen has with you
Writes your praises more times than I’ve ever spoken them true
I see how my pen looks at you
Writes the taste of you on pages
While inking out her proclamations
I’m jealous
Jealous my pigment doesn’t stain

Blankness to tell
Your story
Jealous I'm not words and sound and syllable
Holding space in the atmosphere
Like a reservation booked
Where you are
I am but a poet
Whose pen has made
Me her handmaiden
Tale

Talkin Shit

See?
I love that shit called Us

We be bad
Muthafuckas

Nah I can't shut my mouth
I gotta say it

Ya know
Ima parley it

He's a righteous soul brotha
He ain't no jive turkey

He ain't tryin to hurt me
But puts a hurtin on me

He wanna butter my bread
On the black hand side
From the back hind side
When he
Sliddddddes
That thang to me
I explode like

Dy-na-mite

He gives me that get right

That Daddy Ima act right

I bless him right back
Wit that
Grip tight

Kitty got lock jaw
Call it cat fight

Break him off summa of this
Ohh baby I need this
In my life

And just like most black folks
Our Sundays are for praising
And when I see that steeple
Raised
I get on my knees and hum
A glory filled hymn

Say Amen

Can I get a witness
I wanna baptize his thickness
Catch his Holy Ghost

While I swallow his Scriptures
I'll probably convert
My Religion
To The Church
Of Gettin it In

But don't save me
I don't wanna be saved

Let him bow his head
between my legs

Prey
I am
And he's the predator
Erasing the memory
Of my past man mistakes
I call him my Editor
the Publisher
Of this New Edition of me

I'm his Candy Girl
And the world
may never know

How many licks it takes
To get to the center
of my tootsie roll

That’s privileged info
And he ain’t tellin

I bet the neighbors got a hint tho
Cause I be yellin
And my skin be glowin
Ain’t said nuttin to nobody
But they be knowin

Yo man ever make you
 feel so good
It makes you swear
And cuss?
Mine does
Cause that’s
Why

 I love that shit called us
Yeah We be bad muthafuckas

Black Majick

He casted a spell on my walls
Turned my yoni into cauldron
Waved his wand
And stirred until
Black Majic
Happened

Hocus pocus
He focused
On my erotic colloquialisms
Until he had me mastered
Gathered my ego's ambition
With his alabaster
And casted her
With his
10th power to the Sun
Conjured me to cum

Deep hard strokes
Divinated his rod
To my water
He Found my well
And drank my spills
Well

As I chanted
His name
Spirits gathered
Escorting me beyond the veil
To the realm where snatched
Souls dwell
With his touch
He warlocked
my body
Summoned my pleasure
In waves unmeasurable
Between Moon and Heaven
my waterfalls
Splashed
To the conducting of his
Voodoo hands
More deity than man
He has
My lips parting in
Offering
My mouth
A vessel for
Idol worshiping
Life altering

And each time he commanded
I levitated
Sawed my body in half
And pulled rabbits out my hat

Orgasmically

Every climax
Tricking my body
Teasing like it would be the last
But endlessly
My chakras assembled
Like a scarf
That he pulled
Through my
Spine
Through my
Mind…
Effortlessly
I was
Aligned

A possession of my body that
Inhabited parts of me so
Deeply
An exorcism is
Required to
Release me
My head spins 180
He makes my
Tongue
Speak differently
Splits my personality
The power of his Lingam

Compels me
To Houdini my body
Escape this Reality
To
Ride with a Dragon
And swallow his fire
With no mortality

He casted a spell on my walls
Inscribed his name
In manuscripted movement
Revealed ancient language
Written in my cells
Decoded that
Which
what was once
Encrypted

He's gifted
In the dark arts
When the lights go out
My legs spread apart
Only to reappear crossed
Behind his neck
I can't escape his lustful hex
Keeps me anticipating what's next
Thrown nuts and bone
Foretold my future
Ima cum outta context

Emptied of my contents
Exsanguinated
Drained
Renamed and
Rebirthed
Emancipated
Of my Body…
Earthed

Watershipped

Pour a libation
For the dearly departed
Soul that escaped my
Lips in a whisper of your name
Moans mourning the loss
Of consciousness
Of awareness of time and space
Say some words over my body
Your heat turning my flesh to ash
in the wind
manifestation
Ask and it shall be done until Blessed
Be
pleasure raging in my veins
Explosive like a aneurysm
Your essence is my life support
Vent your frustration on my throat
With no regard to esophageal tendencies to get
choked up on long syllables
I'll swallow what I've heard
Pour a library
Into my mouth
And these hips will write you books
Recite the alphabetical order of your DNA
Just pour something

Smooth for me
Cause I
have a nasty secret fantasy
I want you
to spit for me
open my legs and grab
my hips for me
we both can part our lips
If you let the water drip...free

Tell me to open my mouth
And my jaw lowers like a moat
To taste your salivary essence
Is my hope
I wanna taste
mouth watering as you gather
the write words and let them spill into
my oral cavity
Once a taboo
Now a crave
Your lips
Made me your slave
Your ways are
the Gahtdamn that broke my back
my mountains arched towards the heavens
I touched the sun
and you shined right back
that night we signed an erotic contract
My soul elevated so high

when you puffed your lips
against my clit
the angels caught a contact

You must've been smoking LaLa
Had me moaning like Ahhh ahhh
got me so high I witnessed rain
falling from above the clouds
The puddles formed silently
But the splashing was loud
Your kiss much sweeter nowandlater
I crave to taste the flavor
pooling in the recesses of your mind
I wonder if you got the time...
today
to meet me in the bedroom
Your liquid silk
held in reserve
I wonder if you'll spit
For me
I want my mouth
Watershipped
With Words

Nasty Rewind Revised

I wanna suck your dick
while you spit poetic lines
On my knees as I search
Into the depths of your eyes and say
mmm *** rewind
And as you go back to recite those words you rehearsed
My tongue finds your balls and licks them in reverse
Use your Lingam against my mouth like a muzzle
Silence my moans
only thang heard is my throat guzzle

I'm feelin extra greedy
My entire mood on fuck you feed me
When you stroke transcendental
drill hard -don't go easy
I was made for you so I can take it
You was made for me
that's why we're Naked
Thirsty for that good water
I want to drink it
I'm like a squirrel lookin for that buried nut

And with the stroke of my hands you'll probably give it up
Consider yourself wholly devoured
I won't need to take that long but
I could do this for hours and hours
My mouth comes with a trigger warning
If I use this tongue gun your cum will
Come pouring
So act accordingly
You can be the star of this porn I'm recording
See, I look sexy with you in my jaws
And a good performance deserves
Some applause
So clap my cheeks and let your fingers snap
I'm a poet too so let me run these verses back
Your body is the stage and your dick is the mic
Put my name down, I wanna get on it tonight
Oh- it's a slam you say? Perfect cause I enjoy you for three rounds anyway
But this ain't no real competition
I just wanna spit poetry while in my favorite position
Let my words wash over you saturate your face and sheets
From 6 to 9
My throat and your kids have a formal meet and greet
And I hope you're not diabetic cause you are what you eat

my sweetness just might raise the numbers of
your A1C
Aye I see how you lookin at me
like I got that strange
My juicy fruit got you crazy and yo snickers bar
got me deranged
scribble scrabble Your thoughts
Diggin deep like you gettin religion
And givin praise
when you're stroking between the scriptures of
my legs
Love when you tongue tie my clit
It always leaves my grace amazed
And for anyone confused
Its mo betta than just sex
My mind gets him rock hard
And his mind gets me drippin wet
We got that soul connection
Cause of our bomb ass intellect
Evryone in the audience can gaze at us with hate
or admiration
either way we're still a beautiful and dope
collaboration
Like Slim and Thick, Bey and Jay or Bonnie and
Clyde
And if you ever forget what this mouth do Baby
Just say
***Rewind
And I gotchu like you got Barz

And you got me like a parking lot got cars
We go good together and together we go good
Some wanna try to write me off
But a bitch never could
My metaphors are sick, infect their system like coVid
And they got no sense or taste yeah them crows stupid
Some wanna try to write you off but they don't understand
Everything about you gave me amnesia bout them
Harpo who's this man?
Infinity stone snapped em right out of existence
Nothin more than bad memories
With a fuck boy's persistence
you draped those gems as beads around
Me more powerful than a Thanos glove
We do this shit yes this is what we does
Cause ain't nothin more poetic and sexy
Than the Just us of black love
We rock hard for each other
Flames of the twinning kind
And when this lifetime ends
We' will simply say
Universe *** rewind

Wonderings

I wonder...
I wonder if he knows
That the little moles
Under his left eye are like
A constellation
So every time I look at his face
I get a confirmation
That I'm stargazing
without
Ever looking at the skies
He even has the nerve
To have Moons in his eyes

I bet
I bet he doesn't know that
I think he's a planet
A necessary body in my Universe
His breath a nebula that's catches
My attention and heart in the same hand
And reigns supreme in my alignment
His absence a black hole
That has me feeling like
an Alien that needs to phone home
Saturn Rings
And He answers

My Orbital Assignment
Rotation around
The sun
In 3..2..1

I want to tell him I love him hardest in my silence.
A space I pour all of him until he fits me like a mold
No room to ever cram words
He fills my capacity to all that it can hold
Forces me to grow
Then gives me more
Keeps me wondering what's in store
Like a Black Friday shopper waiting at the door
I've waited in time's line
To claim him as mine
Hello
Was it
Me?
That he was looking for
when he traced his finger from my temple to the axis of my mouth
Down to yoni's door
Smile hanging in the balance of my happiness
Aiming for his heart with arrows shot from my Cupid's bow
Sagittarius with Libra tendencies
He's into me

Poem Home

He said I was his poem
Sprawled me on his blank sheet
Pulled my legs into a perpendicular phrase
Draped them around his neck and told me the shoes stay
on
Then he wrote me
Found his voice inside my words
Line by line
He laid me
Bare and vulnerable
Feelings raw
Made me swear and cuss
Formed me in his mind then contorted me into sentences
Written to make nuts bust

Spoke me into lofty places, heels to the ceiling
His ink became my erotic sexual healing
I am the result of his sensual mental synapses
Spokenword to which the angels fingers are snappin
In my stanzas he deeply buried his passion
When he spit me I could feel his ink splashing

And when he slammed me the thrust came
crashing
I am sounds orated through dimension
Expression of lyrical intentions
He makes me magic
Was the poltergeist to my soul when he spoke
through my static
I cum in couplets and my metaphors are
orgasmic
I can't imagine not being in his life
He didn't have to ask
I volunteered to be his wife
His ride or die
I'm always at his right
My existence is indebted to his scribe
Because I don't become this me
until he begins to write
Strokes of pen
Become strokes of him
I am consumed
By his plume
Until he finds the end of his quill
Immersed in the deepest parts of my
Real ness
He has given me his rib and breathed spirit into
my nostrils
I'm the Eve of his freedom
He runs wild with me

Gripping my wrists until he has dominated me in every genre
Given me a perfect pentameter pulse
Gifts me immortality as to audience ears I boldly cross
To him I'm never lost
He knows where to find me
Hears me when I call to him
Sometimes
Sees me even when he's looking into her eyes
He'll never leave me
Unless it's all on the stage
But I'll always return to his page
After all
Poem is Home

818

818
He makes love to me like he's been here before
Knows my body like
He's Been my body
Like we were a nucleus broke apart and he needs
to get inside of me to be himself again
My lover you have erected a flag on newly
charted territories
I am the bounty in your treaty
You own parts of me no one else has ever agreed
to see
I touch myself in your voice because you make
me be the best parts of me.
I submit to your will.
I melt in the heat you shine on me.
I become ready with hunger to take your light
To claim the light that you give,
so intensely, that I cast it as my own
I shine you so brightly I am believed to have
fooled some to think I have a light of my own
Moon magic
When you touch me I feel the pull of oceans to
the sky
DNA being asked back
To its Source

You command me like you created me
Resurrection in the palm of your hand
You can pull my life through all these little deaths
And I come out on the other side
Exploding in multidimensional ecstasy
Birth

Eternity Evermore

Its been one thousand ninety five days
Any way I say three years
It's spelled
Eternity

The time it feels I waited
To have you next to me
Me next to you
Where've you been
I needed you

Was living life in a Nietzche poem
Unchained Earth away from from her Sun
God had died
You were the
madman
And I lost you

Couldn't find you living
In the life
I was living
Our breadcrumbs eaten
By those that found us
Yes to what was un inconvenient
To what made the hurt of missing you

A little less depleting
Otherwise
All of my blood would have
Spilled in pain
What else could cure the Insane?
Is that why I'm still so crazy about you?
Quiet the whisper of Wind
Always swirling
Just behind my ear
My name Whispered on your
Soul's lips
Shhhhhh
Don't say it

Unuttered it's a vibration sent
Via ancestral drum
Heartbeating in my
Head
A thought thumping in your chest
It was Love
Seeking

The lilt of your poetry
Sounded
Like the lean of my lips
I knew our kiss would
Taste like a memory

Would taste like
Hey Me
Would Taste-
Like
Honey
Combed with
The electricity
Of your energy

Days are light years
And we live them together
Sometimes
Apart
But never Separated
Our intentions will keep us
Together
Even if perforated
By distance
Through Dimensions
Or If necessary otherwise
at least to
Meet you Again
However
I can't wager those chances
I need this to be forever
This time!
I want my Right now to be my
Evermore
Only this and nothing More

We can stop counting now
Because infinity has no numbers
I trust you with us
As I trust
I with us
There is no I in us
We've found We
I love you

www.ingramcontent.com/pod-product-compliance
Lightning Source LLC
Chambersburg PA
CBHW051734130826
49812CB00033B/860
9789357442916